D0888043

# The Great
# <u>Wall Street</u>

# RETIREMENT
# SCAM

## FIRST EDITION 2010

# The Great
# Wall Street

# RETIREMENT
# SCAM

## What THEY
## Don't Want You To Know
## About IRAs, 401ks
## and other plans

### By Rick Bueter

LegacySafe Publishing

## Publishers Note:

This book is for educational purposes only and does not provide legal, tax or investment advice. Readers should consult a professional before acting on any of the information contained within. Any references to outside sources have been edited for clarity's sake. Information is from sources believed to be accurate but is not warranted.

© 2010 Ricard Paul Bueter
Published by LegacySafe Publishing

All rights reserved. The text of this publication, or any part thereof, may not be reproduced in any manner whatsoever without written permission from the publisher.

Printed in The United States of America

Second printing, February 2011

IBSN    978-0-615-36663-0

LegacySafe Publishing
c/o The Bueter Companies
9820 Willow Creek Road, Suite 410
San Diego, CA  92131

(858) 621-9099

# Contents

# About This Book

For several years, I have been thinking about writing a book like this. It was clear after the market meltdown in 2009 that it could wait no longer. The decade ending in 2010 left millions of Americans wondering how they will ever retire, and why the system they placed their trust in has burned them.

Those who are close to me know that I definitely have opinions, but opinions based on reality. I am not a follower. If that makes me a little bit of a renegade, I am fine with that. It's time to call a spade a spade. Millions of Americans have lost their retirement dreams because of Wall Street and government agencies.

During the writing process, I spoke with clients and friends about what they would like to see. The general consensus was that it should be simple, short and to the point.

Almost everything people receive from a financial professional is written from an attorney's point of view. We have enough of that in the world. So, there is no legalese here.

This book was not written for professionals. It is not meant to be technical in any way. It is written so that <u>anyone</u> who has their life's retirement savings invested in a financial market can understand how it relates to the ultimate goal of creating a secure pension. You will find this writing to be more conversational style, as opposed to a "how to" book. As such, I have taken some liberty with grammar, punctuation and form just to make it easy on the eyes and to make points when needed.

Few people have a lot of time these days to read a 300-page novel, so I have kept it short and to the point. It's about helping those who are lost at sea with their retirement savings to get a bearing on which way to sail and move forward. Anything more technical would diminish the points found here. If you desire more details, take what you have read and find an expert who really understands what I have written here. The more knowledge you have, the more equipped and in control of your future you will be.

Within the book there are a few websites referenced. Be sure to visit each one. For me, they were eye opening to say the least, and I am a professional. They help explain a lot about the Wall Street system of retirement. After you finish reading, you may also be inclined to write your Congressman. Do it. I call and write my Congressman at least 4 to 5 times a year. America is going through a historic change right now, and everyone needs to stand up and be heard.

If you have found this book to be helpful, pass it on and tell others about it. Send an email to friends recommending they read it. Buy an extra copy for your kids. Most people just don't have the knowledge about money and retirement that is in this book. Many are afraid to ask for help or don't know where to go. Help them. That's what friends are for.

You can find me online at:

**Website is www.rickbueter.com.**

**Facebook** – The Great Wall Street Retirement Scam

**Twitter** @rickbueter

Email **rickbueter@pacbell.net**

My personal life consists of my wife Kathy and our four children. Kathy has the patience of a Saint. Thank you Kathy. When I am not speaking or meeting with clients, we travel as a family in our motorhome throughout California and the Southwest.

Rick Bueter
March 29, 2010

P.S. I would like to thank Dick, Gloria, Bruno, Tony, Garry, Jim and especially my father Terry. Without his 50 years of experience in retirement planning and encouragement, this book would not have been written.

# Preface

THEY cannot guarantee you an income as long as you live.
THEY won't even use the word pension in their investment plans.
THEY aren't telling you THEY don't have the solution to guarantee retirement security.

Who are THEY?

THEY are the ones who have created the Wall Street system of retirement.
THEY are responsible for the outcome of your retirement security.
THEY wrote the rules of the system.

Millions of American workers and retirees have participated in a retirement system they trusted to take care of them until the last days of life. With the most historic stock market decline since the Depression, the realities of that failing system were recently unveiled. That system is known here as the "Wall Street System of Retirement." It is the retirement system in which millions of Americans have invested the financial security of their retirement years. Unfortunately, this is also the system that has caused a substantial number of those retirement savers to lose their financial security for retirement.

There is another system of retirement that has avoided all losses, preserved retirement dreams and secured them with guarantees of income for its participants.

It is a system that has existed for over a century and has proven itself over and over again, including times when Americans found themselves in the most challenging economies. Even in the Great Depression, this system delivered on its promises.

It has always been and will always be a system that provides millions of Americans certainty, guarantees and financial security. It is known as The Insurance Company System of Retirement.

**THEY**, the creators of The Wall Street System of Retirement, are determined to keep the truth from you, the retirement saver.

# Chapter One

# It's All About Income

During the decade of the 90's, you could open almost any newspaper or magazine and read about the mutual fund of the year posting double-digit returns. The advertisements to invest on Wall Street were everywhere. It was a time when America's retirement workers were euphoric about their 401k, IRA and other retirement plan investments. How easy it was to become mesmerized by the investment returns on 401k account statements and lose track of what the higher purpose of those numbers represented.

Then in 2000, the tech "bubble" burst.

For many investors this was the beginning of a long forgotten lesson about risk on Wall Street. The stock certificates which retirement savers thought were sound investments became worthless pieces of wallpaper. Those who worked in the technology field saw substantial declines and many incurred total losses of their retirement savings. Like a spinning top wobbling and about to tumble over, this bubble was a sign of how vulnerable financial markets were coming to their disastrous end.

In 2009, the system finally collapsed with the largest market meltdown since the Great Depression. Investments evaporated under the eyes of the most intelligent CEOs and government officials. Even the regulatory agencies with mission statements of "investor protection" failed to protect investors. It was a financial virus caused by a lack of knowledge, appreciation and understanding of the risks on Wall Street. There were so many unacknowledged risks that something had to buckle, and it did.

Today Wall Street is trying to regain integrity and trust as the right way to invest.

But, invest for what?

Is the goal to invest in the most popular mutual funds or stock of the day? Is it really about investing for retirement? I ask that question because few retirement savers really understand the ultimate goal of retirement investing. Perhaps it is because the goal really isn't clear or the goal was misrepresented. Or, maybe it's because Wall Street does not have the solution needed to create financial security in retirement.

Wall Street is a giant and powerful propaganda-marketing machine. Not only have they decimated the retirement dreams of millions of Americans, they have in the process caused those retirement savers to lose focus on the real goal of retirement savings.

This goal cannot be overstated.

**Guaranteed Income For Life!**
**Guaranteed Income For Life!**
**Guaranteed Income For Life!**

No matter what system you choose to save and create your retirement pension with, it's all about income - guaranteed, 100% certain income.

These words should be focused on in such a way that you cannot possibly be distracted by any other concept, thought or strategy.

Whenever you look at your retirement account statements, think about those words.

Pick apart your retirement investments and see exactly how this objective will be achieved. As you read in future chapters, there is a good chance that you will see how you will not achieve your goal. In fact, if you are one of the millions of Americans investing in the Wall Street System of Retirement, there is a high probability you will not achieve that goal at all.

## It's All About Income.

You can't sustain your life without *it*.
You can't live without anxiety unless you have *it*.
Without *it*, the choices you have until the day you die are limited.

## The Missing Link

As ridiculous as this may sound, millions of American workers have no idea how they will create the income that will sustain their lives when they get to retirement. It's not their fault. The system of retirement in America has not shown them how to do it. The system is all about investing the money and the dazzling choices, formulas and schemes to invest. It is not about the goal of a secure income guaranteed for life.

Retirees are now finding out that the strategies they used to grow their retirement savings are not working. Many find themselves running out of money at a time in their life when they cannot go back to work.

Again, it's not their fault. It's the fault of the system they participated in. The retirement system in America is in crisis mode, and it is only going to get worse.

This book has been written to point you in the direction of how you are going to sustain your life in the final years of living. Because, when it's all said and done, the only thing financially that matters in retirement is how much income your retirement savings will create. This assumes you still have a retirement savings when you need it.

## Confusion Abounds

There are strategies everywhere about creating income, especially today when bank interest is near zero. Retirees are trying to figure out what to do with their Wall Street portfolios. Others are talking about higher taxes in the future. So, what should you be thinking about? <u>Guaranteed income payable for as long as you live.</u>

Think like a lottery winner for a moment.

Imagine that you just won the lottery, and you now have a check that is going to pay you large income payments for the rest of your life. Because the income is guaranteed by the state, you have 100% confidence that those checks will be there every month. Every year you receive more than enough to pay your bills.

With that set of circumstances, do you really care too much about taxes? Do you care about what happens with the financial markets? Do you care about investment strategies? Do you really care about how much money you have, as long as you have all the income you need? The answer is probably "no." All your basic needs of living will be met as long as you live.

4

Now that you are thinking like a lottery winner, start asking yourself questions such as:

- How can I create an income with the certainty and security of a lottery winner?

- How will I grow my retirement savings with confidence and certainty so that when it is time to create income I will be able to receive the maximum amount possible during the rest of my life?

- How will I protect my lifetime of savings from financial markets, political uncertainty and world events so that I can be assured of uninterrupted lifestyle security all throughout retirement?

- Do I really want to be a "retirement investor" or a "retirement winner" and create a secure retirement income guaranteed for life that I don't have to worry about?

*It's All About Guaranteed Income For Life.*

# Chapter Two

# Your Parent's Pension

To understand what THEY don't want you to know, you must understand what has happened to the American retirement system over time.

During the time following the Depression in the 1930's until 1974, America had a retirement system that worked well. It was a system where people didn't worry much about their retirement income. They weren't concerned about financial markets. This is because they were guaranteed a secure retirement income from their employer. It was called a pension. This put great confidence into the lives of those working toward retirement as well as those already in retirement benefiting from the steady income they were receiving.

The retirement system of their day was simple and worry-free. It did not require the assistance or fees of a credentialed financial planner or stockbroker. In fact, it was a retirement system where the employee was not responsible for any of the investment decisions. The lack of anxiety from financial matters concerning retirement was a great benefit of this system.

The very calculated nature of your parent's form of retirement plan provided an employee the security of knowing exactly what their retirement benefit would be from the time they started with a company until the year they retired. They knew precisely what the benefit amount at retirement was because they received a statement each year that told them.

At retirement, they would receive that pension check guaranteed for the rest of their lives. This type of retirement planning is called a defined benefit plan. It is named this way because you know exactly how much you will receive at retirement, hence the term "defined."

Since there were no IRA or 401k plans during this time, American workers used tax-deferred annuities issued and guaranteed by insurance companies to further supplement retirement income. Funded with after tax contributions this created another guaranteed fund with guaranteed growth that could be turned into retirement income if needed. This need was served easily through a life insurance agent. Retirement security was never so simple.

## The Post Depression Retirement System – Defined Benefit Pension Plans

Until 1974, the defined benefit pension, referred to here as "your parent's pension," was the primary retirement system in the United States. As you read above, there were substantial benefits to the employee in terms of time, guarantees, and less anxiety about financial matters. This type of retirement planning has certainly served the needs of millions of Americans.

Let's take a look at why this system worked so well.

Your "parent's pension" plan targeted a specific retirement income from the day the employee began with the company. It created instant security about what would happen when the employee retired 40 years into the future. There was no guessing about what the pension income benefit would be upon retirement.

It was professionally managed. A highly educated and experienced professional pension manager, not the employee, managed the investments in the company plan. This manager was managing the money for thousands of employees, ranging in age from young employees in their 20's to those in their 60's and beyond.

Your "parent's pension" plan had a very long-term investment time horizon. Since it may have been up to 40 years or more until some of the employees would retire, the pension manager could make very long-term investments without much concern about market fluctuation or economic cycles. Anticipating the pension needs of future employees, a 100-year investment timeline was a normal course of professional pension management.

There were economies of scale that greatly reduced risks. When an employee retired, a lump sum of money was carved out of the pension fund. Since there could be thousands of employees continuing to work, this lump sum used to create the retiring employee's pension would be a very small percentage of the entire pension fund. Most likely, the amount used to fund the employee's pension was less than one percent of the entire pension fund. On the contrary, in a typical 401k, the employee must take all of their savings to create a retirement income.

Each year a pre-calculated pension income would already be established for those employees who would retire; and, as part of the pension manager's responsibilities, they would know how much cash to have on hand each year for this purpose. With such a coordinated pension process, the manager could time the retirement distributions of the pension plan without the need to sell investments at a loss.

During the 1940's to the early 1970's the Depression was still fairly fresh in the minds of the financial community. Businesses of that day wanted to take care of their employees and provide them with the highest degree of certainty and security with their pension. Companies also wanted to remove themselves from the risk of paying the employee a pension for the next 20 to 30 years or longer. So, the company pension managers turned to the only solution that held those characteristics.

They did not give the money to banks, as a bank does not have the ability to provide a guaranteed income for life. They did not give the employee's pension money to Wall Street, as they also do not have the ability to guarantee a pension for life. Even if banks and Wall Street could guarantee a check for life, the Great Depression had left painful scars about those financial institutions in the minds of Americans who were seeking financial security. Therefore, it was to a life insurance company that the pension manager turned over the lump sum of money needed to create a guaranteed pension for as long as the employee lived.

## Why A Life Insurance Company?

Life insurance companies are in the business of guarantees. They understand how to provide both guarantees at death (known as life insurance), and guarantees for longevity, (known as pension annuities or immediate annuities).

Life insurance companies are businesses of integrity, not greed. Policyholders may never get rich, but they do sleep at night. It is a completely different type of financial institution from almost every angle.

This is what American businesses wanted for their employees back then. It's also what American lawmakers wanted for America during the post-Depression period.

The defined benefit plan paired with The Insurance Company System of Retirement was a system that worked.

Today, millions of retired Americans are confidently receiving their pension checks from insurance companies. As it relates to their pension they have absolutely no concerns about financial markets, political matters or world events. They will get their check, guaranteed for the rest of their lives. The Insurance Company System of Retirement worked.

It's the system THEY, The Wall Street folks don't want you to know about.

*It's All About Guaranteed Income For Life.*

# Chapter Three

# The Great American Retirement Experiment

The 1970's began a period of great challenge for Wall Street firms. During the 1960's, Wall Street had seen tremendous growth in business, but it was in 1969 that a serious business contraction hit the industry. There were bankruptcies, mergers and receiverships of Wall Street firms. Substantial amounts of customer money was lost or tied up in lengthy legal proceedings. [1]

There was a tremendous loss of consumer confidence, and Congress was concerned about a possible "domino effect" involving otherwise solvent brokers who had substantial open transactions with firms that failed. This is surprisingly reminiscent of today's debacle and the sub-prime mortgage market.

Wall Street was becoming desperate, and Congress needed to act soon. Even other types of businesses were having their challenges. The financial markets were weak, and solutions were needed to regain consumer trust. Wall Street responded with discounted brokerage fees and no-load mutual funds.

But, Wall Street was still looking for a solution to regain footing and needed a catalyst to get the American investing public to start investing again. They found their answer by lobbying Congress.

---

1 *Validity, Construction, and Application of Securities Investor Protection Act of 1970*, 23 A.L.R. Fed. 157, 179 (1975).

## The DIY (Do-It-Yourself) Retirement Program Begins in 1974

Through heavy lobbying by Wall Street and businesses, Congress changed the retirement tax laws of America. They launched a new set of retirement plan rules called ERISA, the **Employee Retirement Income Security Act.**

There were dozens of detailed changes with ERISA, but there are two that are critical and require a close look.

The first is that of the vesting rules for Defined Benefit Plans, the type of plan referred to in Chapter Two as your "parent's pension." The rules were changed so that an employee could receive a retirement benefit without the need to work nearly their entire life for the same company. This became a major challenge for pension managers who needed to restructure portfolio investments since benefits needed to mature sooner. Investments with a shorter time horizon also caused diminished investment returns.

The shorter investment time horizon and shorter vesting schedules placed greater challenges on businesses. They now found that they had to put more money into a retirement plan at a time when the business environment was not very good. This was a disincentive for businesses to want to create secure pensions for their employees.

The second and most noteworthy aspect of ERISA was that it was the beginning of the Do-It-Yourself (DIY) retirement system, also known as the Individual Retirement Account (IRA). To get Americans to buy in to the new DIY retirement system, Congress created the incentive of a $1500 tax deduction for the very first IRAs. This new retirement system, called a "Defined Contribution

System," would require lots of explanation. Americans now had to learn how to invest for retirement on their own.

So, who would step up to help Americans navigate their way through this new pension program?

Who was desperate to find a new niche opportunity that was perfectly positioned to guide uneducated American workers with these new laws?

Who had the financial solutions employees would need?

It was Wall Street. Indeed, Wall Street could not have been happier.

It was a new beginning for Wall Street and the key to regaining the trust of American investors. It was the spark that gave Wall Street the answers for which they were looking. They were now able to market to every American worker and help them fund their own retirement with stocks, bonds and mutual funds.

## Wall Street Blocks The Competition

After experiencing the profit potential from fees earned on self-directed Individual Retirement Accounts, Wall Street wanted it all—without competition. THEY wanted to be THE system that would control the lifetime of retirement savings Americans would build. They knew that, without a level of control, retirement savers would naturally choose the security of a bank or an insurance company to grow their savings. Those choices would cut Wall Street out of the opportunity to charge the fees those firms so aggressively sought, since most retirement savers would choose guarantees over promises and ideas.

Again, Wall Street lobbied Congress.

## The 401k is Born

In 1980, Wall Street found their answer to becoming the gatekeeper of the American worker's retirement savings with the 401k plan.

After the successful launch of the Individual Retirement Account (IRA), Congress implemented the 401k. Now Wall Street could set up shop right at the employer's doorstep. This would give them control at the paycheck level using automatic payroll deductions. They knew that creating the tax incentive at the employee level and providing a turnkey system for businesses would be a powerful sales proposition for both the employer and employee.

It became very clear through the tax incentives written by Congress that this was the way Wall Street intended for Americans to save. As time progressed, higher contribution limits were set for the 401k that exceeded IRA contributions. This clearly was a benefit for Wall Street, steering the money toward them and the retirement solutions within the 401ks they provided. The Wall Street 401k successfully blocked banks and guaranteed insurance annuities as investment options for American workers.

Part of the 401k program was that employers were allowed to give employees company stock to fund their account. If given a choice, the average worker would have never invested in that particular stock had they not worked at the company. In fact, it's possible they might not have invested in stocks at all. Nonetheless, the provision to fund an employee's 401k plan with company stock was an attractive solution to cash strapped companies, and large numbers of American workers were betting their retirement dreams on it.

Funding a 401k with company stock turned out to be a huge disaster for millions of Americans. Enron was probably the most well known company to disappoint their employees who had invested their life's savings in its 401k funded with company stock. These were people who worked a lifetime and lost it all in a flawed system they trusted to create retirement security. There are hundreds of other stories just like Enron.

## The Bull Market Of ERISA

The twenty-year period from 1980 – 2000 was the longest running bull market in history. Economists say the substantial rise in the markets was a result of economic growth. Undoubtedly, there is a lot of truth to that. However, the correlation between ERISA and the 20-year run in the markets cannot be overlooked. These new sources of investment funds spurred increasing demand for stocks that caused the prices to go up. The tech bubble and bust of 2000 illustrated that much of the market's gain was artificial and not based on fundamental business principles.

In **Figure 1** you can see that the Dow Jones Industrial Averages were volatile from 1960-1980.

Massive speculation in stocks occurred during the early 70's only to be followed by a serious market decline again in late 1974. It's important to take note of this, as American retirement savers investing on Wall Street never had the experience of a bad financial market until the beginning of the twentieth century. It's quite possible that had Americans owned IRAs and 401ks throughout the 70's their experience from those volatile years might have diminished their enthusiasm for the Wall Street system of retirement. Even if investors had been presented with the chart from Figure 1 during the bull market of the 80's and 90's, they might have tempered their investing style. But, that is something THEY wouldn't have wanted anyone to see. A picture is truly worth 1000 words.

You can see on the chart at Figure 1 that the market floundered during the 70's. But, things changed in the late 70's and into the 80's. In 1980, businesses were implementing the first 401k programs.

As shown in **Figure 2**, the correlation between Americans plowing their retirement savings into the ideas of Wall Street investments and the growth in value of the financial markets was obvious. Even at a time when short-term interest rates topped over 20%, the Dow Jones Industrial Average was in growth mode until 1987 when the first major market correction of this period occurred.

There were many benefits of the capital formation that occurred during the 80's and 90's. Technology made great strides and substantial wealth was created from the new personal computer industry. It truly was the greatest bull market in history.

But, was it a bull market created by economic growth? Or, was this great bull market of the 80's and 90's fueled mostly by too much money chasing too few good businesses?

The answer is probably the latter. In the late 90's, the meaning of the saying "irrational exuberance" (coined by Alan Greenspan) was about to be unveiled. By the end of the 90's, there was clearly too much money chasing too few stocks and the bubble burst in 2000.

During the 90's, many Americans held jobs in the right place at the right time with technology firms and millionaires being created out of low wage earning employees simply because they acquired stock in their 401k plans. For many, this was the first time they had ever experienced numbers like this on their personal financial statements. Although many of these millionaires thought they knew what they were doing, most were completely unprepared to manage the wealth and the risk. They thought this could last forever.

What they didn't realize is that they had only won the lottery, but still needed to cash the ticket before the time ran out. Many of these employees did not diversify their retirement holdings. So, when the tech bubble burst in 2000, the stock lost value and they lost their millionaire retirement dreams. You can see the effect of this in **Figure 3**.

The outcome of The Great Retirement Experiment that started with ERISA in 1974 is that fewer Americans have enough to retire on. It is becoming painfully clear that the cost of retirement will be far higher than anyone has predicted in the past. Medical, taxes and energy will all cost more. As a result, America is headed for the most severe social problems to affect our aging population in the history of the country.

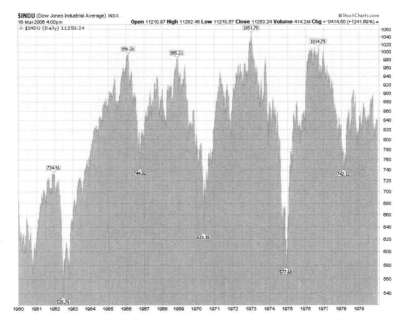

**Figure 1 The Dow Jones Industrial Average 1960-1979**

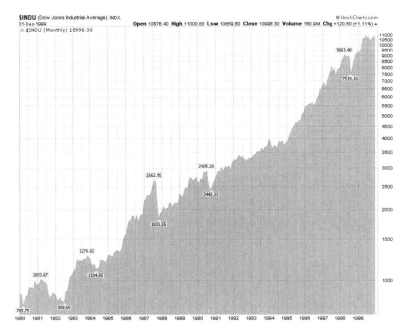

**Figure 2 The Dow Jones Industrial Average 1980-2000**

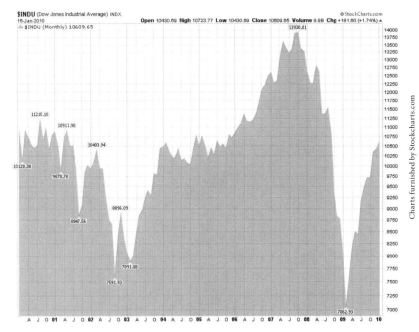

**Figure 3 The Dow Jones Industrial Average 2000-2010**

*It's All About Guaranteed Income For Life.*

# Chapter Four

# Why The Average American Is Doomed To Fail On Wall Street

For nearly 40 years, Wall Street has done such a successful job at brainwashing American retirement savers that nobody has seen what is actually going on. Once you truly understand the task at hand (to create a guaranteed income for life) and the resources to accomplish that task, the risks are enormous.

In almost every magazine about money THEY promote themselves as retirement investing experts, promising that your retirement dreams will be realized if you give them your money. If you turn on the television there are financial channels that promote Wall Street managers with their ads and interviews. Even at selected sporting events like golf, Wall Street is working hard to make Americans believe their system of retirement savings is the only one. To all of you who are saving in this system, you are being duped!

It's not your fault, though. You trusted the system the government put in front of you. Since 1974, you have been fed the propaganda of the Wall Street marketing machine. For nearly everyone, the Wall Street 401k and IRA is all they have ever known. But now it's time to understand why it didn't work so you can make the right decisions. It's time to act so that you can avoid total poverty when you are in the very last years of your life.

Many people who believe they know what they are doing are fooling themselves. As you will see, the 401k rules position the American worker at such a disadvantage that success is nearly impossible.

## The Challenge - You Are Now A Pension Manager

Congratulations, you are now your own pension manager! With the change to the Do-It-Yourself system and 401k plans, you are now in charge of your own retirement. You are responsible for the successful creation of a pension income to pay yourself an income upon retirement for the rest of your life.

There are only two things to be concerned about during the next 40 years:

1. Invest your money wisely and don't lose any.
2. Create an income with that money which you will never outlive, just like your parent's pension did.

Here are the rules…

1. Your investment choices will be limited to Wall Street products, not FDIC insured accounts and insurance company plans like your parent's pension income.
2. Any gains or losses within the limited investment selection offered by your employer will be your own responsibility.
3. The mutual fund company is not allowed to tell you that "it might be in your best interest to get your money out of the markets."
4. The mutual fund will charge you whether you make money or lose money.
5. You cannot move your money outside of your 401k to a retirement pension solution more suitable until you are of retirement age or leave your job.

6. You will not be given any financial solutions to guarantee that your 40 years of savings will create a secure pension upon reaching retirement.
7. Any education on investing, advanced portfolio management or other technical courses must be paid for by you.

Imagine if it was your first day on the job as an electrician and you get shocked because you don't know what you are doing. This is exactly what is happening to millions of American workers. Unfortunately, today most Americans are beyond shock and now just numb because of the economic disaster.

Think about this for a moment. The risks are huge. They are much higher than even a professional pension manager faces. It's no wonder millions of Americans are being forced to give up their retirement dreams.

## The Odds Are Terrible With Wall Street 401ks and Wall Street IRAs

With your 401k, you have been asked to do the job of a highly trained professional pension manager. Let's look at some of the technical angles where knowledge of pension management is required. Think back for a moment to our discussion about the pension manager for your parent's pension. You are being asked to do the same duties that manager did for your parent's pension, yet with both hands tied behind your back.

## Time Risk

A professional pension manager responsible for large numbers of employees may use an investment time horizon of 100 years. That time element enables them to absorb the volatility of economic cycles and financial markets. It also enables them to earn higher returns because the investments are able to realize their full potential.

You don't have 100 years. All of your money must mature at a single point in time: retirement.

## Market Risk

The American worker who retires must take their entire 401k and create income with it. A professional pension manager only needs to withdraw a tiny portion of the entire plan to create the employee's pension. If only one retires, the withdrawal of that one employee's portion of the pension fund won't even make a dent in its value.

If the financial markets decline when the 401k investor retires, the results are not going to be positive. This is exactly what millions of American retirees have just experienced. You just don't have the same advantages a professional pension manager would have. Because you must create a retirement income using 100% of your personal pension assets, any economic risk, market event, political event, and even acts of God can affect the value of your account at retirement. This can substantially diminish the income you expected to sustain your retirement lifestyle.

## Education Risk

If you did not receive your advanced degree in retirement investment management paid for by Congress, you are not alone; nobody has. Yet, when the Do-It-Yourself system was created in 1974, Americans were thrown into this system and had to invest their life's retirement savings in IRAs and 401ks with no knowledge on investing.

As demonstrated in the recent historic market decline, many professionals and bank CEOs did not realize the risks on Wall Street. This fact alone should be ample proof that the Wall Street system of retirement has unimaginable risks, even to the so-called "financial gurus." Do you really want to risk your retirement dreams in something like that?

## What About Guarantees?

There are no guarantees in the Wall Street 401k system. NONE.

If your mutual funds cause your retirement dreams to be lost, Wall Street will not replace the money. Your Wall Street advisor will not make up the difference in losses if your investment evaporates. That's just the way it works on Wall Street – no guarantees. **But THEY don't want you to know that.**

Think about everything we have discussed here. Compare the tasks you must manage perfectly compared to those of a professional pension manager. Today, the American retirement saver just doesn't have the resources nor circumstances to achieve success with any degree of certainty.

## What Are You Investing For Anyway?

The misunderstanding about 401ks is that there is no predetermined retirement income benefit. When you reach retirement, there is no specific dollar amount that you will receive as a pension guaranteed for life. What you will receive as retirement income is a complete mystery. Look at any Wall Street 401k brochure and see if you can find information about creating a pension guaranteed at retirement. Chances are you won't find any. That's because your 401k cannot guarantee that.

If that is the case, why would any logical person work for 40 years, sacrifice to save, and think this system of retirement would create a secure income guaranteed for the rest of their lives? The answer is they wouldn't if they understood what THEY don't want you to know.

The Wall Street 401k system puts the responsibility for success or failure 100% in the hands of the American worker without giving them the education they need to be successful pension managers.

Even the system of becoming a licensed driver in America has more accountability than creating financial security in retirement. There, you must study, take a test, learn how to drive and then purchase insurance in case you make a mistake.

### *It's All About Guaranteed Income For Life.*

# Chapter Five

# Wall Street's Solutions For Secure Retirement Income

Let's take a look at the typical retirement income solutions THEY might suggest and uncover why these "solutions" fail.

You will see, when compared to your parent's pension, they all come up painfully short. Many people will run out of money before they get to the end of their lives. And remember, these are Wall Street solutions so there are no guarantees.

## The Systematic Withdrawal For Income

One retirement income solution promoted by the mutual fund companies throughout the 90's was the systematic withdrawal plan. Under this strategy, you sell shares of your mutual funds each month to create a specific income. The intent was that your mutual funds would grow over the long term and that not only would you create a secure income, you would also create secure growth. That didn't work.

Those who were presented with this strategy as a way to create a secure retirement income were on a course to run out of money. The systematic withdrawal method assumed that markets would always move up. In looking at the irrationally enthusiastic investment returns of the '80s and '90s, one could have easily interpreted the systematic withdrawal as a viable option.

During the period 2000-2009, the weaknesses of this strategy became increasingly apparent. In order to maintain the same monthly income, retirees had to sell more and more shares of their mutual funds each month. This is because the values of stock index funds experienced a dramatic decline during this period. Retirees who followed this strategy rapidly depleted those shares along with the value of their mutual fund investment.

For many retirement investors, this strategy caused them to run out of money before the end of their lives.

## Living Off Bond Fund Interest

Many investors have looked to bond mutual funds as the answer to their long-term retirement income needs. There are two concerns here if creating a guaranteed income for life is the goal.

The first concern is that income from bond mutual funds is not guaranteed and that it can fluctuate. When you are in retirement and working within a monthly budget, this can become a challenge when your income goes down.

The second concern is market risk and loss of principal. As interest rates go down, the value of your investment can go up. But as interest rates go up, bonds go down in value as will your investment. At the time of this publication, interest rates are at historic lows. In fact, rates are probably the lowest most people will ever experience in their lives. So when the rates do go up, bond mutual fund investors may experience the biggest market losses in history.

This is what THEY don't want you to know.

## Buy Dividend-Paying Stocks

Another income strategy is to buy dividend-paying stocks and live off the income.

The strategy says as the company increases its profits, the dividends will go up and investors will be able to increase their income in the future. But what if the company can't raise its dividends? What if it has to lower the dividends? What if the company must stop paying a dividend? What if the company goes out of business?

Companies who pay dividends know that investors are counting on them to pay a dividend every quarter without fail. When a company which pays a dividend has to reduce it or stop paying it, shareholders typically will sell their shares and the stock experiences dramatic declines. An investor not only loses their income, they may also lose the investment in the stock, which could represent an entire life's retirement savings. This is not an attractive situation when you are 70 or 80 years old.

## REITS Sound Good

Another strategy is to buy REITs. REITs stands for Real Estate Investment Trusts.

These are stocks that invest shareholder money in the real estate business. They generally pay an income like bond mutual funds. The income is not guaranteed and is dependent on the profitability of the companies held in the fund. The income on REITs can fluctuate from something to nothing. It is all based on the management of the REIT, the profitability of the real estate businesses held within the fund and economic conditions.

Another type of REIT is called a non-public REIT. These are similar to a limited partnership in that, when purchased, you generally cannot take your money out until the officers of the company determine it is time to give the money back to you.

## The Misconception About Retirement Income

One of the biggest misconceptions about how to create retirement income is causing American retirees to miss out on living their lives to the fullest.

When you look back at how your parent's pension was created, the company pension manager nurtured that pension money until it was time for the employee to retire. To achieve the maximum income with the maximum certainty for the employee at retirement, the pension manager purchased a guaranteed lifetime income annuity with an insurance company. Had they put the money into bonds, stocks or other instruments, they would have not been able to achieve the certainty of income and the security of that income.

The misconception created by Wall Street is that a secure retirement income comes from interest and dividends. As you can see from the previous paragraph, there is no certainty of future income with Wall Street solutions. When creating a retirement income this way, many retirees are shortchanging their lifestyles when they should be living their lives to the fullest. In many cases, the alternative of creating a pension income with an insurance company results in substantially more income. It also results in the highest level of certainty and guarantees.

But, THEY don't want you to know about this because THEY would lose the profit made from fees they could charge you over your lifetime.

There are dozens and dozens of other Wall Street "strategies" we could discuss, but the most important point as it relates to your retirement dreams is that they all come from the Wall Street system of retirement. None of these come with what your parents had.

### *It's All About Guaranteed Income For Life.*

RICK BUETER

# Chapter Six

# How THEY "Protect" Your Retirement Security

Since 1974 and the creation of the Do-It-Yourself IRA and 401k by Congress, Americans have trusted their government to provide a retirement system that would protect them in retirement.

Considering all of the layers of government officials supervising the retirement system, it is hard to believe that an American worker who saves for 40 years in a 401k or IRA could have absolutely no guarantee of a secure pension. But, this is exactly what is happening, and it is all a result of the retirement laws enacted by Congress. To understand how this could be true, let's take a look at how The Wall Street system of retirement works.

## The Securities and Exchange Commission (SEC)– The Chief Enforcers

Congress created the SEC in 1934 after the stock market decline of the Great Depression. They are empowered by Congress to maintain orderly financial markets and to regulate Wall Street. The SEC on their own can set the rules, policies and procedures to carry out their responsibility charged by Congress. They are responsible for the system by which Wall Street operates.

They have the following statement on their website www.sec.gov,:

> *"As more and more first-time investors turn to the markets to help secure their futures, pay for homes, and send children to college, our investor protection mission is more compelling than ever."*

There is that word "protect" again.

In financial matters, how can anyone be protected when there is no guarantee? It is comical that in the Wall Street system the word "security" is used as the word for something that holds absolutely no guarantees. Stocks, bonds, mutual funds and all other Wall Street investments should really be called insecurities.

When we want to protect something financial, we insure it. Insurance is purchased because unpredictable bad things happen. For example, the Federal Deposit Insurance Corporation protects banks when they fail. Nobody plans on a bank going out of business. In fact, when the bank first opens, that is the last thing on the minds of its founders. It's just that things happen in the world that no one can imagine. That's why banks have insurance.

The banks pay premiums to the FDIC for this coverage. If a bank fails, the FDIC is an insurance fund to guarantee the deposits to the bank's customers.

It's the same for life insurance companies and the premiums their policyholders pay for annuities and life insurance. People buy life insurance because they *know* they will die, just not when. Because their death would be an economic loss to the family, they buy economic protection in the form of life insurance.

For those worried about the possibility of outliving their income, retirement savers purchase pension annuities. The risk of running out of money is shifted to the insurance company when an immediate income annuity is purchased. The annuity insures a payment will be made as long as the annuity owner is alive even if they live to be over 100.

## Oversight of The System

Every mutual fund, stock and bond is filed using a prospectus with the SEC. The SEC does not approve or disapprove of the investment, they just make sure everything about the risk is fully disclosed. Mutual fund companies and brokerage firms that hold 401k plans and IRAs are accountable to the SEC for their operations. The SEC also conducts audits of Wall Street firms, and they are supposed to weed out problems.

In 2008, the largest "Ponzi" scheme in history was discovered. It had been going on right under the nose of the SEC for decades. In December 2008, Bernie Madoff was arrested and pleaded guilty to stealing billions in this scam. This was a person who was audited and part of the Wall Street system. Every decade, there are dozens and dozens of scams like this going on right under the nose of the SEC that cause Americans to lose their life's savings. It's the same system millions of Americans have invested their life's savings in.

So, who is responsible for overseeing the SEC?

Within Congress is a group of lawmakers called the House Financial Services Committee. The chairman of this committee is currently Barney Frank. This committee is responsible for laws that govern just about every financial organization in the country. Banks, Insurance Companies, Wall Street and many other types of financial interests come under their lawmaking jurisdiction.

Within the Financial Services Committee is a subcommittee that is directly responsible for the Securities and Exchange Commission and FINRA.

Visit the House Financial Services Committee website at www.financialservices.house.gov to view a list of members. Make a note of the members who are a part of these committees. These are the Congressional lawmakers who are shaping the financial system in America. In the next chapter, the business, politics and influence of the American retirement system will be unveiled.

## Financial Industry Regulatory Authority (FINRA) – The Local Financial Police

FINRA is a non-government owned corporation empowered by the SEC to supervise, regulate and monitor the activities of Wall Street firms. Think of this organization as the local Wall Street advisor police. Essentially, they enforce the rules and policies of the SEC at the retail investor level. They have the power to assess fines for misbehavior by brokers and create policies, procedures and rules of their own to carry out their responsibility empowered by the SEC. FINRA is also responsible for the training, licensing and sales activities of stockbrokers. Bernie Madoff was one of these stockbrokers.

FINRA is responsible for supervising every aspect of securities and mutual fund sales within IRAs and 401ks. It is FINRA's job to create a system of integrity. In fact their website boldly states:

> *"FINRA is an independent regulatory organization empowered by the federal government to ensure that America's 90 million investors are protected."*

Notice the word "protect" again. Everybody in the Wall Street system is always trying to protect you. If 90 million investors just experienced the most historic market decline since the

Depression, who are they protecting? It surely doesn't seem like they are protecting the average American who has their 401k and IRA invested in that system.

Another key concern of FINRA is making sure that an investment is suitable. Ironically, if the primary objective of the American worker and their 401k or IRA is to create a retirement pension that is guaranteed for life, the question becomes how mutual funds, stocks or bond funds could be a suitable investment considering they have no such guarantee within them. I suggest to you that it depends on whose attorney defines "suitability."

In the minds of the average American worker, the desire is a guaranteed pension for life, regardless of what happens politically or economically. If presented with the question about suitability as posed above, most would likely find a suitable investment to be one that comes with guarantees. Those come from the system of retirement THEY don't want you to know about. That system is The Insurance Company System of Retirement.

*It's All About Guaranteed Income For Life.*

RICK BUETER

# Chapter Seven

# Money, Power and Greed – The Politics Of Retirement in America

There is one question that explains everything about the politics of your 401k plan choices.

## "Why isn't an FDIC insured account part of every American worker's 401k investment options?"

When you finish this chapter you will understand everything you need to know about the politics of the Wall Street system of retirement.

There is a daily battle going on in Washington D.C., and it is a fight over who will be the financial institutions that get access to the American worker's 401k and IRA savings. It is being fought behind closed-door meetings at the highest levels of government and through lavish fundraisers for Congressmen who seek to maintain their office at the next election. What you will learn as you read on is that the lawmakers involved in this are being influenced by financial organizations on Wall Street with unlimited amounts of money to spend.

In Chapter Three, you read how the system changed after Congress opened up (and exposed) the retirement savings of Americans to Wall Street through IRAs and 401k plans. Another type of retirement plan used by teachers, medical professionals and municipal employees is called a 403b plan. Recent law changes have now restricted the investment options for 403b plans under the guise of "protecting" the worker. Regardless of who is doing the lobbying to control those dollars, the American worker has become the victim of even more government control.

As mentioned earlier, it is Congress who mandates the laws that determine the features of our retirement plan options.

## Conflicts Of Interest – Follow The Money

Although this is not a surprise to some, there is a conflict of interest among the lawmakers responsible for American workers' retirement plan options.

As mentioned in the previous chapter, the House Financial Services Committee oversees the investments of Wall Street, including those held in both IRAs and 401ks. It is their responsibility to present new laws to members of Congress that relate to issues of financial matters.

At this very moment, The Financial Services Committee is reviewing all kinds of ideas to figure out how to restrict and control the American worker's retirement savings even more than it is today. All of this lawmaking is being done under the guise of "protection."

Congress has the ability to mandate an FDIC insured account or a guaranteed fixed annuity as one of the 401k options all employers must offer employees. **But, why don't they?**

## Where Are The Guarantees?

In the recent financial market meltdown, nearly all American workers who had their life's savings invested in 401k plans had no guaranteed options. For almost everyone, there was no way to move and protect their money in anything other than Wall Street securities. Billions of dollars and decades of savings evaporated.

Even money market mutual funds touted by Wall Street as the safe money account in retirement plans became vulnerable to losses. These funds were promoted to employees as a "safe" money investment option in workers' company retirement plans because their share value was expected to never fluctuate in value. Without an Emergency Act to put a temporary safety net in place ordered by President Bush , the money market funds of millions of Americans would have experienced catastrophic losses.

Imagine now what was going through the mind of American workers who had their life's retirement savings invested in a 401k during the market meltdown in 2008. It was like being inside a burning airplane without a parachute. There were no options; but, there should have been.

## Why Don't American Workers Have An FDIC Insured Account In Their 401k?

During the market meltdown, nearly every 401k participant wanted to make their money safe but had absolutely no way to do that. What if they had an FDIC insured account as an investment option? What if they had an insurance company guaranteed account as an option? Wouldn't that have been a suitable investment to have during the most historic market decline since the Great Depression? Of course, it would. Why doesn't that already exist? Politics.

The mutual fund companies make their money and stay in business by charging fees on your investments. They get paid whether or not you make money. Imagine what would happen if Congress mandated that every American worker have an FDIC insured account within their 401k plan. Think about what every worker would have done during the market meltdown to protect their life's savings. Many would have moved their money to the FDIC account.

**That move would have caused the mutual fund companies to lose the fees they were charging on their investment accounts. This WOULD have put them out of business.**

**In plain terms, Congress has protected the businesses of Wall Street by restricting the American worker's ability to protect their life's savings.**

## This is what THEY don't want you to know.

The retirement savings of American workers was severely jeopardized in the market meltdown because Congress did not find it important enough to mandate the security of any insured investment selection within the retirement plans of America's working class. Even after the meltdown, there is no mandated guaranteed or insured solution leaving the American worker vulnerable to the next market disaster.

## Now Follow The Money

Congress did not mandate a guaranteed account option within retirement plans because of politics. Go back to the House Financial Services Committee members website at www.financialservices.house.gov and make a note of the members of Congress who sit on those committees. Now take a look at the states they are from. Look at who the head of the House Financial Services Committee is and what state that person calls home. It's Massachusetts.

The northeast corner of the United States holds some of the largest mutual fund companies in the country. These are major league Wall Street firms. They have a serious interest in earning fees from the trillions in Wall Street mutual funds. They also want to make sure nobody can take away the turf on which they do business. Now let's take a look at how the business of retirement savings plans in America really gets done.

## Where Greed, Power and Money Meet

www.Opensecrets.org is a non-profit group that tracks the source of funding for political campaigns. Take out the notes that you made of the members of the Financial Services Committee and look at who is giving them money. Look up the chairman of the committee and review the history of contributions. Take note of the contributions in the years 2009-2010.

You might not immediately notice that one of the top 5 contributors to the Chairman's campaign was one of the largest mutual fund companies in the country. That is because they have covertly abbreviated their name by using initials instead of the company name that Americans would immediately recognize. In fact, this company almost has a monopoly on the retirement savings of Americans.

It is a documented fact that lawmakers regularly take money from Wall Street firms as you can see at Open Secrets. That influence is determining the choices you have in your 401k. At the risk of losing political contributions and the power of their office, members of Congress find it more important to protect the interests of Wall Street than they do the 40 years of life American workers will give to create their retirement security.

Now you know how the system works.

You know why you don't have choices that could protect your retirement security.

And now you know why THEY don't want you to know.

*It's All About Guaranteed Income For Life.*

# Chapter Eight

# 401k Advice – What Advice?

Have you lost money in your retirement savings?

Did you think you had a secure plan for retirement?

If the answer is yes to either of these questions, this chapter may explain why this happened to you.

FINRA (The Financial Industry Regulatory Authority) oversees every aspect of how Wall Street firms do business with the public. In order to understand the system of retirement Wall Street provides, you must understand the training, methods and delivery systems of that advice to appreciate why your retirement plan has failed. We will start with a basic understanding of the typical 401k plan and then discuss the system of advice outside of company sponsored plans in Chapter 9.

## The Wall Street Advice System– 401k Participants

How do you intelligently choose 401k investments? Do you really know where 100% of your money is invested at all times? How can you take full responsibility for your retirement future if you don't know?

It's not your fault that you don't know.

Mutual funds are only required to tell you what is held in their funds on one day of the year when the annual report is sent out. They don't have to tell you where your money is on the other 364 days. This is all that the Wall Street system requires. Remember, you are supposed to be the pension manager of your own 401k and IRA. How could you possibly be fully responsible for your money if you don't know where it is invested at all times? You could own Enron, or General Motors (both worthless stocks today) and not even know it. Mutual funds are really a kind of blind trust. You invest the money, but you really don't know where all of it is until you see the annual report.

In nearly all company sponsored defined contribution plans like 401ks and others, the Wall Street firms that implement the plan use their own proprietary mutual funds. Out of those funds come fees that are deducted from your account whether you make money or lose money.

When you only have a choice of one mutual fund company's group of funds, diversification among funds may be misleading. Even when you think you might be diversifying your 401k by having more than one fund, many of the stocks and bonds within the funds overlap one another.

To illustrate this point, think of two mutual fund managers that manage different funds at the same company. It is common that both end up picking the same stock. So, when you think you are diversifying your investments, it is many times an illusion because you may own the stock in both funds and not know it.

Most 401k plans and even IRAs may offer only one family of mutual funds to diversify with. This means that the philosophy of money management all comes from the same company. If the portfolio managers make their stock selection using all of the company generated research resources and their money management philosophies are wrong, everyone goes down with the ship. That could be really bad if your company sponsored retirement plan only has funds from one mutual fund company. That is lack of diversification at its finest.

## What THEY Don't Want You To Know About Mutual Funds

What THEY don't want you to know is that THEY will never tell you when you should move your money out of the markets.

First of all, if you did take your money out, THEY would lose the fees.

Secondly, it's not their responsibility to tell you when to take your money out. So, they will never tell you in either good times or bad what you should do. That would be advice, and legally they are not allowed to give advice. They can only take your money and invest it. So whose responsibility is it? It's your responsibility. But how would you know?

You probably would not know because that is how the Wall Street system works. In fact, you will most likely be the last one to know. That's when it's usually too late, and the bad news is already out.

Now if THEY were really trying to "protect" you THEY would put in bold letters

**"THE OUTCOME AND SUCCESS OF YOUR RETIREMENT INCOME IS YOUR RESPONSIBILITY. THE INVESTMENTS WE HAVE GIVEN YOU TO USE OVER THE NEXT 40 YEARS MAY OR MAY NOT BE GOOD ONES. THE ASSURANCE OF A SECURE RETIREMENT INCOME FOR LIFE IS NOT GUARANTEED. THERE ARE OTHER OPTIONS BUT WE ARE NOT REQUIRED TO TELL YOU ABOUT THEM."**

Think about that statement for a few minutes if you are a 401k or IRA investor on Wall Street. I rest my case.

*It's all about guaranteed income for life.*

# Chapter Nine

# The Real Cost Of A Wall Street Advisor

You might be saying to yourself, I have an advisor and lost money in the financial markets. How could this have happened?

As mentioned earlier, a suitable investment to create financial security in retirement would be one aligned with the guarantee of an income for life either now or in the future. So, let's take a look at why your advisor may not have provided this for you.

We begin by taking a look again at the Wall Street system.

Everything about the advice you receive from a Wall Street licensed advisor starts with the SEC, then FINRA. All of the philosophies about money management, the formulas, the investment choices for securities, the training for advisors and the types of advice all derive from these organizations. Once an advisor is in the system, it almost becomes a religious experience as it's all about the amount of fees that are generated in the system. That's what makes it run.

A Wall Street firm charges as much as they legally can because THEY are accountable to their shareholders, not you. Because of that, in the mind of an advisor, there are no other investment options but the ones THEY offer. Those that are offered are the ones that create fees for the firm. They will get paid whether you make money or lose money.

If you have lost money it is because of the system.

There are 2 basic kinds of advice you get from the Wall Street advisor.

## The Salesman

Commissioned financial advisors are paid to only sell investments to the public.

As an advisor licensed by FINRA, they are not trained as portfolio managers. The only qualifications their license empowers them for are to be able to take orders to buy and sell securities. Here the salesman (also known as the advisor) receives an up front commission for this service. They are not paid to monitor your investment or take any responsibility for the successful outcome after they have received their commission. They may contact you to sell, but this is not advice as technically their compensation is for the transaction, not advice. This type of relationship occurs with mutual funds, non-public REITS, limited partnerships and all types of other securities.

At one time, the energy company Enron was an investment in many portfolios but has since gone bankrupt. Brokers who sold this stock to clients had no responsibility other than to sell the stock. That is technically where their responsibility ends. When the bad news became public, it was too late. In this type of relationship, it would have been your responsibility to call your broker and tell them to sell.

A FINRA licensed advisor is not required to have an advanced education in pension portfolio management to receive a stockbroker license and work with the public. That means that although they can talk about stocks, bonds and mutual funds, they are not required to understand the technical aspects of creating and maintaining a pension fund. In fact, millions of

Americans have turned over their retirement savings to FINRA licensed stockbrokers who have no experience as pension managers.

If the goal is to create income guaranteed for life out of your Wall Street 401k, IRA or other retirement plan, wouldn't it be logical that you would want the expertise of a true pension manager? This would be a pension manager who understands the unique needs and risks of creating a pension income guaranteed for life, not someone whose only qualification is that they hold a license to sell you stocks, bonds and mutual fund investments.

But that is something THEY don't want you to know.

## The "Monitor" Advisor

The second type of advice is where an advisor charges a fee to select outside money managers to manage your money.

This type of advice can make the most sense <u>if</u> you choose to participate in the Wall Street system of retirement investing. In this advice relationship, an advisor will seek out a highly trained money manager who will manage your money by diversifying it in mutual funds or picking individual stocks.

There are some important facts to understand about stocks and mutual funds.

First, there are no guarantees with either of them. Secondly, with mutual funds in this scenario, you will be paying fees on top of fees. Mutual funds have an internal fee, and then you will pay an additional fee to your advisor for putting you in this scheme. Unless justified by the risk-adjusted performance of the advisor, it is a losing proposition. For those who have never discussed risk-adjusted performance with their advisor, that is another thing THEY don't want you to know.

## Here are some more considerations THEY don't want you to know.

There is no safety net here. These advice systems come from the Wall Street system of retirement investing with no guarantees. If all the formulas and economic models fail, you will go down with the ship. The Titanic was supposed to be incapable of sinking. The Wall Street system of retirement investing all comes from the same place. It starts with the greed of Wall Street that influences Congress, which controls the Securities and Exchange Commission who oversees the Financial Industry Regulatory Authority.

You will only get advice on what the system has to offer. What if gold coins are a better place? What if privately held real estate is better? What if CDs at credit unions are better? (Remember the high rates in the 80's) What if insurance companies are better? If Wall Street cannot get paid on it, you won't hear about it. You only get advice on what the system has to offer even though there might be a better solution outside of the system.

## Remember It's Your Money

Just like going to a doctor and seeking treatment, it's your body, and you have the final say. Wall Street has their ideas about what to do with money, and they all favor Wall Street, not you. If you are uncomfortable with investing, don't do it. If you lose money, your broker is not going to put it back into your account.

If you place your retirement security with someone you call your friend, you must decide if this is business or personal. If you put the financial future of your life in the hands of a friend, do they really understand the magnitude of the responsibility they hold? Are they going home at night thinking about your financial security in retirement or theirs?

Many people have lost money because they thought the Wall Street advisor knew what they were doing. Many advisors took risks with their client's money that even they had no understanding of. These risks became apparent only after the client's money had evaporated. To evaluate the real cost of a Wall Street advisor, you must also factor in any losses they have created on your behalf.

Remember the retirement mantra from Chapter One.

*It's all about guaranteed income for life.*

**If you begin with that premise, all the answers about how to create a secure retirement pension become clear when you seek them.**

# Chapter Ten

# The Retirement System THEY Don't Want You To Know About

American retirement savers who have been a part of the Wall Street system of retirement have had a wake up call to say the least. During this past decade millions of retirees and pre-retirees have had to go back to work or make serious reductions to their lifestyle. However, the worst part of The Great Wall Street Retirement Scam may come near the end of their lives. It is the number one concern of those in retirement today when it comes to household finances. That concern is running out of income before you run out of life.

The solution to this has always been there. It's just that THEY have not told you about it.

## The Insurance Company System Of Retirement

It is a secure system of retirement that has existed for over a century.

It is a system based on integrity, guarantees, certainty and financial security. It is not a system based on greed, promises, ideas or strategies. Those individuals who have discovered this system have protected their retirement dreams with guarantees. They have created certainty of their future income, and they have also put confidence in their lives through that certainty.

Because of all of this, they have greatly enhanced the quality of their retirement years.

## Why They Don't Want You To Know

A political battle for the retirement savings of Americans is being fought between the fee hungry institutions of Wall Street and insurance companies. This battle has been going on since the end of the Depression. As you learned in previous chapters, the shift of power to gain access to the American workers retirement savings changed in the late 70's and 80's as Wall Street became the retirement gatekeeper via company sponsored retirement plans.

Since that time, major propaganda campaigns have taken place to dupe Americans into believing that insurance companies were inferior places to save for retirement. Even major media outlets would find reasons to put a negative spin on the guaranteed retirement solutions Americans have so desperately needed to protect their retirement dreams. Much of this came from those with little understanding of how secure pensions are created.

In the meantime, Wall Street firms have continued to skim billions of dollars from the American worker's retirement savings regardless of gains or losses. But, THEY could not deliver the one thing every American retirement saver wanted, a pension income guaranteed for life. That's because those guarantees come from Insurance Companies. They are the only institution that can create that guaranteed growth and guaranteed income for life with annuities.

Let's begin by going over the basics of annuities.

## Annuities - Guaranteed Growth, Guaranteed Income

Many people are confused about exactly what an annuity is. Very simply, think of annuities in two categories. Growth, or Income. We will break down each category of annuity below.

## Deferred Annuities For Growth On Your Money

A deferred annuity is a retirement savings plan where money is placed with an insurance company and earns a rate of return. The amount of return is based on the type of deferred annuity you have placed your money in. No income is withdrawn while it is earning a return, hence the term deferred annuity.

The attraction to deferred annuities has always been that there are no taxes on earnings until income is withdrawn. This tax status created by Congress is referred to as a non-qualified annuity as it is funded with after tax dollars. The benefit of non-qualified annuities is that money grows faster than it could in a taxable account, thus creating the ability to receive more income later in retirement. This tax-deferral attribute is the premise with which IRAs and other pre-tax plans have been promoted. It's just that you do not receive a tax deduction when money is placed into a non-qualified annuity.

### The 3 Types of Deferred Annuities

- Fixed Declared Rate Annuities
- Fixed Indexed Deferred Annuities
- Variable Deferred Annuities

### "Fixed" Declared Rate Annuities

The fixed declared rate deferred annuity has existed for over 100 years. It is very simple. In fact, think of this like a bank CD without taxes. Your principal is guaranteed and your interest rate is fixed for a period of time. At the end of the interest rate guarantee period, the rate will renew automatically either higher, lower or the same.

Because a fixed annuity is a contract with an insurance company made over a specified period of time, they must guarantee a minimum rate of return regardless of what is paid currently. This is how The Insurance Company System of Retirement protects those who participate in their system. All states have a law that requires this minimum interest guarantee to protect policyholders so that their money will grow in value while it is with the insurance company.

## The Fixed Indexed Deferred Annuity (also known as the Automatic Pilot)

When the pilot of an airplane wants to take his attention away from the instruments to focus on other duties, he places the airplane on automatic pilot. The automatic pilot keeps the plane headed on the correct course and always pointed in a safe direction. Today, there is a new type of annuity that keeps your money safe like an automatic pilot. It's called the Fixed Indexed Annuity.

The fixed indexed annuity makes your money grow by automatically capturing market gains when financial markets go up. When markets decline, it eliminates any possibility of loss. All of your money stays safe, thus the term "Automatic Pilot." Like an automatic pilot for airplanes, the fixed indexed annuity keeps your money always pointed in the right direction, up never down.

If you have never heard of fixed indexed annuities (FIAs), one reason might be because they are relatively new. The first FIAs became available in 1994. Of course, another reason you might not know about them is because THEY don't want you to know.

## How Fixed Indexed Deferred Annuities Work

Very simply, interest is credited through a <u>measurement</u> of a financial market index such as the S&P 500. Your money is never invested in any financial market. When money is placed into a fixed indexed annuity, the insurance company takes a note of the current index data point. They note the value of the index at the starting date of your annuity and at an ending point, say one year from now.

If there is a gain in that index over the measurement period, your annuity is credited with interest. Once the interest is credited, you cannot lose it. You cannot lose your earnings, and the interest is compounded. If the financial index does not go up, your entire original principal and any interest are guaranteed safe and secure by the insurance company.

Unlike Wall Street investing, where it's possible to lose your gains, your money in a fixed indexed annuity can only move in one direction, up and never down. It truly is an automatic pilot to keep your money pointed in the right direction at all times. It allows you to forget about financial markets, politics and world events. Fixed indexed annuities make money when markets are positive, and they protect money when market losses are occurring.

The only risk is the amount of interest you will earn. All principal and accumulated earnings are never at risk of loss. Retirement investors who have experienced the benefits of fixed indexed annuities over the last decade have enjoyed growth in their retirement savings from market-linked returns, without any of the historic market declines.

## "Variable" Deferred Annuities

Think of variable annuities as variable principal and variable returns. The benefit of a variable annuity is tax-deferred growth on mutual funds. Until recently, the only guarantees that were available on variable annuities were at death. So, if a financial market meltdown occurred, your money could be guaranteed to heirs at your death. If you wanted to withdraw all of your money, you may experience a market loss similar to owning a mutual fund. As a result of the market meltdown of the 2000s decade, insurers have come up with all kinds of options to guarantee mutual funds using variable annuities.

One consideration of variable annuities is their layering of fees.

Within variable annuities are fees charged on the mutual funds. There are death benefit fees, living benefit fees, administration fees and then fees for other guarantees and options charged to your account value. It is possible for these fees to be in excess of 5%. On a $100,000 investment, this would be $5,000 per year. Over 20 years, there would be $100,000 in fees alone.

Those fees represent years of income for many people. The fees are charged regardless of gains or losses. If you consider the possibility that financial markets may not grow or may lose value, a variable annuity could be a costly proposition. If an annuity has to be turned into cash, the cost of those fees after a period of time could substantially diminish the benefits of the plan.

Only advisors licensed by FINRA can sell variable annuities. This is because the mutual funds inside a variable annuity are securities which must be registered with the SEC. The guarantees come from insurance companies, not from Wall Street.

Variable annuities are evolving and becoming more expensive with the addition of features and options. It would be wise to dig into the details of the fees and expenses if you own or are considering a variable annuity. You will find those answers in the prospectus, some of which are over 400 pages!

## Immediate Annuities For Immediate Income

If you were to ask those who have a pension to define their pension, they would most likely say something like it's a check they receive every month for the rest of their life. Their pension IS an income annuity. In technical terms, it is a lifetime immediate income annuity. These are the annuities referred to as "your parent's pension".

There are several types of immediate annuities. To keep this simple, we will break them into two categories: term certain and lifetime annuities.

A lifetime annuity is created when you give an insurance company a lump sum of money in return for an income guaranteed for the rest of your life. In essence, you are shifting the risk of running out of money in retirement by giving it to an insurance company. If you live to age 120, the insurance company guarantees you a monthly income check. However, if you die prematurely, the income stops just like if you were receiving social security or a pension from an employer. In this case, the insurance company keeps the rest.

Nobody can tell you when death will come. Not even the insurance companies know who will die and on what date. What they do know is that someone will die and how many out of 1,000 people will die each year. Because they know this, they understand how to manage the risk of having to pay someone a check until they are 100 or older. This is a normal course of business for insurance companies, and they have been doing it for more than 100 years.

The other type of immediate annuity is known as a term certain immediate annuity. With this annuity, income is guaranteed for a specific time period usually ranging from 5 to 30 years. If death comes before the end of the period, the payments will continue on to surviving beneficiaries.

One consideration of immediate annuities is liquidity. Once you have purchased the annuity or annuitized an existing deferred annuity, withdrawals into the cash values are not allowed. This is because you have traded the cash values contractually with the insurance company in return for a guaranteed stream of income. Keep in mind that for lifetime incomes that guarantee will last as long as you live.

## The New Annuity On Steroids

One of the disadvantages of an immediate pension annuity is that under a lifetime payout, if death occurs prematurely, the insurance company keeps the balance of the money. This is the way your parent's pension may have worked. This is not a very favorable outcome if you intended to leave something to heirs. We will refer to this as "annuity suicide."

Today, there is a new way to avoid annuity suicide and create a guaranteed income for life without completely losing access to the cash value. We will refer to an annuity with these features as the Annuity On Steroids.

There are three significant features that come with The Annuity On Steroids.

The first feature is that your retirement savings receives a guaranteed growth rate <u>for income purposes.</u> A guaranteed growth rate between 7-10% is not uncommon. This rate of return is used only if you choose a lifetime income. The underlying cash values of your annuity will grow at a rate separate from the rate used for income purposes.

The second benefit is that when it's time to draw a lifetime income, the insurance company will pay you 4-7% of that future value guaranteed for the rest of your life. This income can even be paid over the lives of both spouses so it continues on after the death of a spouse.

The third significant feature of the Annuity On Steroids is that if death occurs before all your cash values have been paid out, your heirs will receive the remaining cash in the plan. If your lifetime income exceeds the cash values, you will still be guaranteed income as long as you live.

For those who want to retain a cash value element and the flexibility to turn the income on or off, the Annuity On Steroids is the solution for maximum growth and maximum income. It also leaves a degree of liquidity should life events change. If you now subscribe to the mantra, "Its all about guaranteed income for life," the Annuity On Steroids is the new age solution for personal pension planning.

## Financial Security Of Insurance Companies

Many people have more equity in their homes than they do in the bank but never think twice about the financial security of the insurance company who would write a check if their house burned down. Insurance companies are in the business of guarantees, not risk and greed. They receive premiums from policyholders and invest those in bonds with the intention of keeping the money safe to pay future claims.

This system of financial management has paid out billions in life insurance death benefits to surviving family members. It has also guaranteed the pension incomes of millions of retirees as long as they lived. From the ground up, insurance companies operate on an entirely different set of ethics and purpose than the Wall Street system.

## The Guarantee Associations

Insurance companies don't take their responsibilities lightly. They know that if there was ever a catastrophic meltdown of their system they could never recover their integrity. As a result there is one more layer of protection for policyholders beyond the guarantees of a company. It is called The National Organization of Life and Health Insurance Guarantee Association (NOLHGA).

NOLHGA is a voluntary organization to which insurance companies belong. It was created to protect policyholders in the event an insurance company suffered more claims or losses than they could absorb.

Some people attempt to compare it to the FDIC for bank deposits, however, NOLHGA is not a governmental organization. If you have never heard of the Guarantee Association, it is not a surprise. Agents are prohibited from explaining it to prospective customers, as there are substantial penalties if it is used as an inducement to purchase insurance. You can learn more at www.nolhga.org.

## The Insurance Company Advice System

The retirement income of millions of Americans has been preserved and sustained by annuities for over 100 years. The advice of The Insurance Company System of Retirement comes from life insurance agents who are licensed by the insurance regulator for the state in which they do business.

Since annuities are one of the primary products of a life insurance company, agents are required to take an initial test and then satisfy continuing education standards to maintain competency. Since creating a guaranteed income for life is the business life insurance companies are in, only a licensed life insurance agent really is qualified to explain these solutions.

## Insurance Company Ratings

Have you ever looked into the financial rating of your homeowners insurance company? Most people never do. However, all insurance companies have ratings to disclose to the public their current financial condition. A.M. Best is one of the leading companies that provide these ratings. Moody's and Fitch are other rating agencies to consider. Generally an A or better rating by A.M. Best is a good place to start.

## What THEY Say About Annuities

As mentioned earlier, there is a political battle being waged for the retirement savings of Americans. The result is huge disinformation campaigns about the use of annuities being carried out by Wall Street firms, the media and brokers. Even those who don't hold an insurance license have wrongly influenced the American worker and retiree about where and how secure retirement pensions are created.

Here are two of the most misunderstood aspects of annuities.

## THEY Say You Can't Get Your Money Out Of An Annuity

This statement comes from those individuals who don't understand annuities and most likely, don't hold an insurance license. It is an irresponsible, uneducated response evoked generally by Wall Street and media types who are insecure about their knowledge of annuities. What this response may refer to is a pension annuity, also known as an immediate annuity. When taken with a lifetime guarantee, this annuity generally does not have any liquidity, and it is true you cannot get your money out once it begins.

However, to make a fair comparison, you do not have access to the money you have paid into the social security system. You will only receive the payments for life. If you are lucky enough to have a pension annuity from your employer, the same holds true. Like your parent's pension, you cannot make withdrawals from the lump sum of money your employer paid to create your pension.

The other side of this is that you will receive a check guaranteed as long as you live. With the new Annuity On Steroids, you can now have a lifetime income feature and liquidity. This overcomes any concerns about creating a lifetime income and losing the money if you die prematurely.

## THEY Say Annuities Have Surrender Charges

This is true.

For the same reason a bank charges a pre-mature withdrawal penalty on a Certificate of Deposit, an insurance company charges a fee called a surrender charge on deferred annuities if you withdraw all of your money before a certain time.

What THEY don't want you to know is that the surrender charge <u>only</u> applies if you withdraw more than the amount that is allowed without a charge. That is referred to as a free withdrawal and is usually ten percent of the annuity value. Using this feature, a withdrawal can be made each year without any surrender charges. Normally, this is enough liquidity for most needs in retirement.

Surrender charges exist to protect the financial integrity of the company and remaining policyholders. When a deferred annuity is purchased, the insurance company makes financial commitments with the understanding that the annuity policyholder will keep their money with the insurance company for a specified time period. With the annuity premiums, the insurance company buys bonds with certain maturity dates. This is how they are able to pay competitive rates of interest on fixed deferred annuities.

If the policyholder liquidates the annuity before the end of the period, the insurance company is protected from losses in the portfolio with the surrender charge. This business practice allows insurance companies to maintain the guarantees they provide to policyholders that do not take their money out prematurely.

These charges are usually waived at death and if a nursing home illness occurs.

**Now that you know what THEY don't want you to know, what are you going to do about it?**

*It's all about guaranteed income for life.*

RICK BUETER

# Chapter Eleven

# 7 Strategies To Guarantee Growth and Guarantee Retirement Income For Life

A wise man once said there are three kinds of people in the world;

> *"People who make things happen,*
> *people who watch things happen,*
> *and people who say what happened?"*

**Decide RIGHT NOW what is important to <u>YOU</u> about financial security in retirement.**

Are you a risk taker and a gambler? Do you find the allure of Wall Street investing attractive? Are you willing to live with the uncertainty of future income that Wall Street provides in return for possibly a few extra percentage points of return? As a reminder, regardless of the return, it's not guaranteed for life. Are you willing to accept the risk that economic and political events will affect the certainty of your future retirement income?

<u>Or,</u> are you someone who wants guaranteed financial certainty and security in the final stage of life?

Do you want to be able to determine what your retirement income will be five and ten years into the future and do so with 100% accuracy?

In order to know where to put your retirement savings, these are the questions you must answer.

It's time to make the financial security you deserve in retirement a reality. It's time to make decisions. <u>Will your retirement security be compromised by Wall Street when the next crisis occurs,</u> or will you have put in place the safety net to avoid that crisis?

**Are you ready to put guaranteed growth into your retirement savings and a guaranteed future income you will never outlive?**

If you are ready, then here are the steps to get you started.

### *Strategy #1* - Transfer Your Wall Street IRA or Previous Employer's Retirement Plan To A Guaranteed Fixed Annuity IRA

Many people don't realize that deferred annuities can be used to fund IRAs. If you have an old 401k or other retirement plan, consider transferring those to an annuity IRA as well. Those who have discovered the guarantees, growth and income options fixed annuities provide have greatly enhanced the quality of their lives. Using an annuity within an IRA is fully approved by the IRS.

When you really think about this, an annuity *is* the most appropriate instrument for an IRA. Think about what creates a secure retirement. It's a guaranteed pension income for life. Only an annuity can provide that. When done correctly, the transfer of your existing IRA to an annuity IRA is tax-free.

### *Strategy #2* - Use An In-Service Withdrawal to Move Your 401k or Other Plan

Are you ready to put some security and guarantees on your 401k? Even if you are working it may be possible to transfer funds out of your company 401k or other plan directly to an IRA annuity.

Many employer sponsored plans allow employees to move money out of the plan at certain ages. It's called an in-service withdrawal. This transfer can be done tax-free.

Doing this would allow you to put the safety and guarantees of an annuity on the money you currently have saved for retirement. If you participate in other plans such as Thrift Savings, 403b, 457, or Profit Sharing check to see if you are eligible for the in-service withdrawal.

### *Strategy #3* - Consider a Pension/Immediate Annuity For Maximum Income Now

Many retirees and those who are just now retiring will run out of money before they die. Their portfolios have either collapsed, or they just don't have enough income to maintain themselves. By converting your retirement savings to a pension annuity, it is possible to substantially increase your income. This could eliminate worries about financial markets, give you more lifestyle choices and provide the retirement security you need today.

If you go back to Chapter Two, your parent's pension was created by the lump sum the pension manager gave to an insurance company. That pension was an income that would pay for the rest of their lives. What many people have been duped by the Wall Street system into thinking is that your income will come from living off the dividends and interest. Unless you are Warren Buffet, that just does not work for most Americans.

### *Strategy #4* - Get An Automatic Pilot (also known as the Fixed Indexed Annuity)

The fixed indexed annuity puts your money on automatic pilot so that when the financial markets move up, so can your money.

When they move down, you don't have to worry. This type of annuity has earned competitive interest during the 2000s decade and protected billions of dollars that might have otherwise been lost had it not been invested on Wall Street.

## *Strategy #5* - Use The "Annuity On Steroids" Feature

The "Annuity On Steroids" feature guarantees you a very competitive growth rate for income purposes and guaranteed lifetime income when you are ready. You can determine exactly what your guaranteed retirement income will be when you are ready for it. If you understand that financial security in retirement is "all about income," the "Annuity On Steroids" is the answer to guaranteed growth and guaranteed income.

## *Strategy #6* - Save With A Non-Qualified Annuity

If you are beyond the working years and have money sitting in banks earning low rates of interest and paying taxes, consider moving money to a non-qualified deferred annuity. With a fixed or fixed indexed annuity you can still have safety and guarantees while growing your money faster. You don't have to take any money out until death, and it can then transfer to your heirs.

One fact about non-qualified annuities that is virtually unknown is that when they are turned into a pension income a substantial amount of that income is tax-free. This is because it is considered a return of your original principal that you already paid taxes on. Annuitizing a non-qualified annuity can make a dramatic difference in income taxes when compared to fully taxable investments.

## *Strategy #7* - Think You're Too Old For An Annuity?

If you think you are too old for an annuity, it's time to change your thinking. Deferred annuities can make sense even for 80 year olds. The safety and security of a deferred fixed annuity when compared to almost anything Wall Street can provide makes sense because of the guarantees.

Unfortunately, the biggest concern when getting older is about becoming ill and needing to pay for nursing expenses. If you have to sell your Wall Street investments to pay for end of life costs, you may do so at a loss. If you needed to liquidate your annuity for nursing home expenses, many companies today allow you to do so without any charges. With a fixed annuity, 100% of the value could be available. There are even special annuities today that allow TAX-FREE withdrawals for nursing home expenses.

**The Older You Are, The More Reasons For Annuities**

As we get older, keeping track of the details becomes more difficult. The final years of life for most people are not the time to take responsibility for managing a stock portfolio. Understanding a 20 page Wall Street account statement is a challenge for many professionals. You can't make your own decisions when you are incapacitated or start to lose your mental faculties. For this reason, money held with an insurance company in annuities and life insurance cash values is one of the most appropriate places to leave it.

When money is with a life insurance company, it is being handled with the highest level of integrity, ethics and purpose. Plus, life insurance policies and annuity policies avoid probate. This makes the estate transfer of these assets easy and free from the legalities of probate.

**Talk To An Experienced Annuity Agent**

If your advisor has never presented you with an annuity as a retirement solution, they are the wrong person to advise you.

Annuities come with many different options. There are issues like ratings, withdrawal features, income features and rate guarantees to consider. Those who are not familiar with annuities and their features are unqualified to talk about them.

Most likely, a friend or co-worker who already has an annuity and can tell you how it has worked for them will refer the right annuity agent to you. Look for a licensed agent with years of experience as the nuances of annuities can vary greatly from company to company. A good agent can show you exactly what you will be able to receive as guaranteed income five, ten and twenty years from now. That is the kind of retirement planning one needs in order to realize retirement dreams.

## Conclusion

If you respect the fact that you only have one life to save for retirement and one chance to get it right, you will appreciate that there is no room for the risk that the government has asked the American worker to bear with their Wall Street 401k or IRAs. If you have been investing on Wall Street, you have experienced those risks.

Hopefully, this book has provided insights about money, greed and the American retirement system that you did not have before. Maybe you have questions about how to make your retirement savings secure with annuities.

Whatever you do, take some action and protect your retirement dreams. If this is the first time you have ever heard about annuities and the guarantees they can provide, consider where you are getting your financial advice.

Remember, it's your money and your retirement. Think about who you are and what is important to you about the balance of life in your retirement years. Think about what is important beyond your money, things like peace of mind, choice, and not being worried about financial markets ever again. That's what annuities provide. That's what The Insurance Company System of Retirement is about.

*It's all about guaranteed income for life.*

That is what THEY don't want you to know.

# Appendix

**Write Your Congressman**
www.house.gov

Until there is change, Wall Street will continue to dominate the American retirement system. If you are in a Wall Street retirement plan at work and are dissatisfied with the investment selection, or would like to get your money out and into your own IRA annuity, send your congressman an email or letter.

Every American retirement saver should have a fixed annuity and an FDIC insured account as an option. Demand that your representative take action on this now.

**Follow The Money**
www.Opensecrets.org

Follow the money trail and find out who is taking money from big Wall Street firms. THEY have an interest keeping outside investment options that can protect you like FDIC insured accounts and fixed annuities out of your company sponsored retirement plan. Let them know you are watching them by sending a letter that you want change.

**Real World Index Annuity Returns**
http://fic.wharton.upenn.edu/fic/Policy%20page/RealWorldReturns-revisedFIC.pdf

Recently the Wharton Financial Institutions Center, an independently managed site at the Wharton School of the University of Pennsylvania, published a paper comparing the returns of indexed annuities compared to Wall Street investments. The results of their research can be found at the above website.

## Insurance Company Rating Agencies

A.M. Best  www.ambest.com
Moody's  http://www.moodys.com
Fitch  http://www.fitchratings.com

# About The Author…

In 1982, Rick Bueter entered the financial planning industry.

He began his training by studying to pass the life insurance agents exam administered by the state department of insurance. After that he studied and took exams administered by FINRA (formerly the NASD) to become a stockbroker and salesman of mutual funds. Shortly after, he took correspondence courses from the College For Financial Planning in Denver, Colorado to become a Certified Financial Planner in 1985. Until 2007 he maintained his status as a CFP. After re-evaluating the content of the CFP program and the use of designations within the industry, he determined that the use of designations did not serve the best interest of the public.

After experiencing the tech bubble of 2000 with his clients, Rick began to question every aspect of the Wall Street system which he was a part of. Elements such as, professional designations, training programs, regulators, the media, financial forecasting models and retirement income strategies were all under care review as they now prompted many questions.

As a professional retirement planner, Rick began to wonder why the long term asset allocation and retirement income strategies marketed to advisors by Wall Street were not working. These models and strategies were hailed as the prudent solutions by the mutual fund industry and the research organizations. He began to question the purpose of the media and recognized that it was really a propaganda tool for Wall Street, not a source of accurate information that a retirement investor could make informed decisions with.

He noticed the media was focused on being a "retirement investor," not about creating a guaranteed retirement pension which is the ultimate goal of saving for retirement. The media interviewed CEOs of companies whose stock had gone from nothing to hundreds of dollars in short periods of time. Even national magazines that were promoted as sources of how to prepare for retirement were steering readers toward the highest performing mutual fund of the day instead of solutions that create secure pensions guaranteed for life. It was like watching a daily horserace to see who would come in first.

It was clear to Rick that the tunnel vision created by the Wall Street propaganda machine was keeping American retirement savers from seeing what was really happening on Wall Street. There was trouble brewing, and virtually nobody saw it coming.

In August of 2007, Rick took note of a news event that signaled something might be wrong somewhere in the financial system. His previous experience with clients during the tech bubble prepared him to be the first man out if there was a prudent reason to get out of the markets. The news event that put him on guard was the announcement by Countrywide Mortgage that they drew all their lines of credit down in one day.

On August 17, 2007, Countrywide borrowed 11.5 billion dollars from the banks they had relationships with. This event was a sign to Rick that something was not right somewhere. That action by such a large organization was not a normal event of business. Rick was now on guard to protect his client's funds that were invested on Wall Street.

By January 2008, the markets were becoming progressively more volatile, and FannieMae and FreddieMac were finding their way into the news in a disconcerting way. This was yet another sign to Rick that something was not right in the markets. One of Rick's research resources was indicating selling volume in the markets was increasing rapidly even though the markets were showing some days of substantial gains.

Another area of concern was that oil was nearing $150 per barrel. In Rick's view, oil was a commodity that had advanced in price much faster than seemed reasonable considering the state of the economy. This was another sign that something was wrong somewhere.

After evaluating all of these market dynamics, Rick knew that the market was about to go into a freefall. In June of 2008, under his advisement to clients, Rick transferred clients who were invested on Wall Street out of the markets. He eliminated the downside risk to his clients' retirement savings. Even though he had no hint of the size of the financial meltdown that was to occur, the action he took to protect his clients' life savings would become one of the most valuable efforts of his career. In the months following and into 2009, the Dow Jones Averages would experience the most dramatic decline since the Great Depression.

The meltdown of the American financial system and the inability of Wall Street to create secure retirement solutions for the American worker motivated Rick to write this book. As an industry insider and licensed stockbroker, he has participated in the Wall Street retirement system and documented his discoveries, conclusions and questions. His experience with Wall Street has made him an advocate of the other system of retirement that has avoided the losses and created permanent financial security for millions of Americans, the Insurance Company System of Retirement.